Wharram Percy

YORKSHIRE

SUSAN WRATHMELL, MA

Wharram Percy, near Malton in North Yorkshire, is the best-known of the Deserted Medieval Village sites. Here the visitor can see the last remaining standing buildings: the ruined church and farm cottages nestling in a steep-sided valley. Ancient trackways lead up onto the chalk plateau where the foundations of over 30 medieval peasant houses can be clearly seen. For forty years archaeologists excavated the site, revealing a settlement which dates back to the Bronze Age, with Roman farms and a wealthy Anglo-Saxon estate.

This guidebook offers a detailed tour of this green, secluded site, explaining the fascinating story of how it was uncovered and what we can learn from the results. Photographs, aerial shots and reconstruction drawings help to bring the village to life.

ENGLISH HERITAGE · LONDON

Contents

3   INTRODUCTION

5   SITE CHRONOLOGY

8   DESCRIPTIVE TOUR
8   The North Manor
9   The South Manor
11   The Peasant Farmstead
14   The Pond and Water Mill
15   The Church of St Martin, the
     Graveyard and the Medieval
     Vicarage
21   The Post-medieval Vicarage, the
     new Farmstead and the remaining
     Cottages

24   SITE PLAN AND QUICK TOUR

24   FURTHER READING

DEDICATION
This guide is dedicated to the Milner
family of Wharram-le-Street, tireless
friends of the excavations, 1950-1990

Published by English Heritage
23 Savile Row, London W1S 2ET
© Copyright English Heritage 1997
First Printed in England by Matthews the Printers Ltd 1996, Reprinted 1997, 2001, 2006
00304 C15 05/06
ISBN 1 85074 6257

Introduction

Wharram Percy is perhaps the best known of all the deserted villages. The name combines two elements in the history of the settlement: a Viking name, 'Wharram', describing the bends in the valley, and 'Percy' - the name of one of the major landowning families in the north of England after the Norman Conquest.

In the Middle Ages, England contained many more villages than it does now. It has been estimated that over 3,000 village sites were abandoned, for various reasons, between the Norman conquest and the eighteenth century. All that may now remain of these 'deserted medieval villages' are the earth-covered foundations of buildings and farmyards. Historical records are patchy, and only careful detective work by archaeologists can begin to piece together the life of a lost community.

Where the deserted medieval village sites have been overlaid by modern towns and villages, archaeologists usually find only slight traces of medieval buildings. Where the sites were isolated from what are now centres of population, much more evidence remains. Here at Wharram there is evidence of the undisturbed sites of medieval farmsteads stretching out in a north-south line along

The first area excavation at Wharram Percy in 1955: a complete house site was being examined instead of digging narrow trenches to follow the wall lines. The archaeologists were surprised to find that below the fourteenth century peasant houses there were the foundations of a twelfth-century manor house, the South Manor. This early photograph of the excavations shows the relationship of the manor house site to the church in the valley (centre) and the roof of the cottages (left). The number of volunteers digging at Wharram rose each year, as the site's fame spread. About 15 camped there in 1953, rising to 35 in 1960 and by 1990 around 100.

the edge of the plateau. Yards and gardens extend behind, and trackways lead out to the open fields. In the valley below, another row of houses, their crofts stretching down to the stream, have been disturbed by later buildings. Some of the building layouts, which are difficult to see at ground level, show up very clearly on photographs taken from the air.

Historical research has shown that the village was reduced to a single farm by about 1500.

Each summer from 1950 until 1990 Wharram Percy village was 'reoccupied' for a short time, as people laboured to discover traces of the vanished settlement. Excavations soon showed however, that the medieval earthworks included or overlay evidence for earlier and more varied human activity.

A plaque mounted on the gable end of the cottages pays tribute to all those who worked here: 'The excavations at Wharram Percy could not have taken place without the hundreds of volunteers and professional archaeologists recruited from all over the world, many of whom returned for successive seasons, and who made Wharram a very special place.'

Maurice Beresford and John Hurst, the excavation organisers, talking to the assembled volunteers in the 1970s.

The last season of excavation: 1990. The Medieval vicarage site

Site Chronology

One of the most unexpected aspects of the research at Wharram Percy has been the discovery of evidence for occupation stretching back to the Stone Age. These notes indicate the type of evidence found, and the part of the site where it was discovered.

Numbers in brackets refer to the tour stops.

c3,500 - 2,300 BC *Neolithic period*
Trees cleared for cultivation: stone axes found in the area, and the hollows left when trees were uprooted on the plateau.

c2,300-700 BC *Bronze Age* Animals kept on the plateau come down to the springs to drink. Pottery found in most of the excavated areas suggest the first settlement was during this period.

c700 BC-AD50 *Iron Age* Two farms established, with associated lines of small enclosures formed by boundary banks. A defensive ditch and gateway, pottery, post holes and gullies near the North Manor site on the plateau (1). Another focus of occupation found near the church, with pottery, bone pins, a brooch and a burial in the valley. (5)

cAD 50-400 *Roman period* At least five farm sites in the neighbourhood by the middle of this period. Masonry reused in a corn-drying kiln, tesserae, (pieces of coloured stone for mosaics) and fragments of window glass found on the North Manor site (1) suggest a villa nearby. Pottery found in all the excavations. A rectangular enclosure, probably a first century farm, shows up on air photographs.

cAD 400-1050 *Anglo-Saxon and Viking periods.* At least one farm survived the collapse of the Roman economy. Two small huts built on the line of the main routeway in the sixth century (1); at least six irregularly spaced farms by the eighth century. Carved bone and antler combs and pins, a copper and iron belt and sword fittings, and thousands of sherds of pottery on the South Manor site (2) suggest that a rich land-owner's house stood here. Weapons and tools were made on the site, and Scandinavian ornaments were worn. A fragment of a stone preaching cross, dated to around AD 800, found in a boundary ditch on the edge of the plateau above the church, is the earliest physical remains of Christianity at Wharram. A corn mill in use by the ninth century (4), and a small chapel on the site of the present church in the tenth (5).

The village was established as a compact group of houses in the tenth or late eleventh century. From this time written records can be used to supplement the archaeological remains.

Eleventh Century *Norman Conquest*
Settlements were organised into parishes. The Domesday Book records that eight ploughlands here belonged to King William, while one was held by Chilbert in return for military service. Each of the two holdings was regarded as a manor. The peasant population lived in family houses set in rows with yards and gardens behind (3); they worked their own holdings in the open fields and also worked the lord's lands. Most of the surviving earthworks are of the eleventh to the fifteenth century.

The first oblique air photograph of Wharram Percy was taken by J.K.St Joseph in 1948. Since then many more have been taken in all sorts of ground conditions. This view looking south, under light snow with a low winter sun, shows up banks and hollows clearly. The village earthworks in the lower half of the photograph comprise house sites on the plateau to the right, and in the valley to the left, each house having a long narrow enclosure behind it. Between the rows of houses a sunken way leads up the valley. In the upper half of the photograph the cottages and the church, the only standing buildings, can be seen on the left, with the mill pond and the stream in its narrow valley beyond.

Twelfth century Manorial records show that the Percy and the Chamberlain families each owned a manor here. Two manor house sites have been identified and called the North and the South Manor (1, 2).

Thirteenth and fourteenth centuries In 1254 Peter de Percy obtained the rights to the manor owned by Henry the Chamberlain. The South Manor house went out of use at this time. The cellar was filled in, the site was used as a quarry, and a peasant farm was built (2). A grant of 1320 mentions a 'park' and 'acre enclosed by a ditch', as well as a mill pond and fishery, and in 1327 Haltemprice Priory (near Hull) was given the right to appoint the priest. The lord of the manor, Walter de Heslerton, died of the plague in 1349, but, after a period of population decline, the number of houses grew to about 30 by 1368 and a corn barn, common oven and a kiln were in use.

Fifteenth century The Hilton family from near Sunderland became owners of the village in 1403 and began to convert the landscape from arable farms to sheep pasture, probably to supply wool to the Pennine clothmaking areas. In 1458 there were still 16 households at Wharram, but the eviction of four families recorded in about 1500, when their houses were pulled down, was the final stage in the desertion of the village.

Sixteenth and seventeenth centuries A single farm remained in the valley near the church when the Hilton family sold the manor in 1573 (6). The manor was quickly sold from one absentee landlord to another and was bought in 1636 by Sir John Buck of Filey whose tenant, John Richardson, was possibly the owner of the fine stoneware vessels imported from the Rhineland and excavated from the seventeenth-century house near the vicarage.

Eighteenth and nineteenth centuries In the late eighteenth century Sir Charles Buck of Hornby Grange in Lincolnshire undertook farm improvements, building a new farmhouse and outbuildings (6). In 1833 Henry, Lord Middleton of Birdsall House, bought the estate and it remains in that family's hands.

Twentieth century In June 1948 Maurice Beresford, lecturer in economic history at Leeds University, visited the valley and isolated church to study the earthworks of the deserted village. The late Lord Middleton gave permission for exploratory excavations in 1950 and John Hurst, a post-graduate student at Cambridge University, began working with Beresford on a research excavation in June 1952. The Deserted Medieval

Village Research Group supported the site as its research excavation, and in 1967 the national importance of the site was recognised when the Ancient Monuments Board recommended that it should be taken into Guardianship by the Ministry of Public Building and Works, now the Department of the Environment. The annual excavations were to continue until 1990, though for only a few weeks each year, and just under 10 per cent of the site has been examined. The results have been published in learned and popular journals, and research continues.

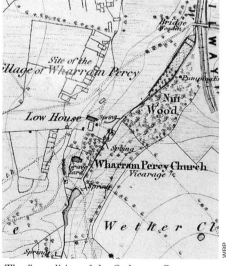

The first edition of the Ordnance Survey map, published in 1854 at a scale of 6 inches to 1 mile. North is at the top. The interpretation of the main earthworks by Captain Bailey in 1850-51 is a remarkable record and the first stage in the scientific study of a site which had been deserted since c1500. The surviving cottages ('Low House') and the church are clearly marked, together with several springs in the valley, and the earthworks of houses and boundaries on the plateau. The site is named 'Village of Wharram Percy', suggesting a local memory of the medieval village.

Descriptive Tour

See plan on inside back cover

1 The North Manor

Evidence for an Iron Age farm, Roman and Anglo-Saxon buildings, and the earthworks of a medieval manorial complex

The 'North Manor' is the name given to the home of one of the medieval Lords at Wharram. They may have lived here occasionally, but the manor was occupied mainly by the Lord's representative, with occasional visits from the owner. Those farming his lands had to pay rents, do special work, and even fight for the lord. In the twelfth and thirteenth centuries two powerful families, the Percys and the Chamberlains, were connected with the village. Both apparently built a residence here, one on this site (now called the

The earthworks of the North Manor

These complicated foundations have not been excavated, but an understanding of the uses of the various parts can be attempted. The layout is similar to standing manorial building groups.

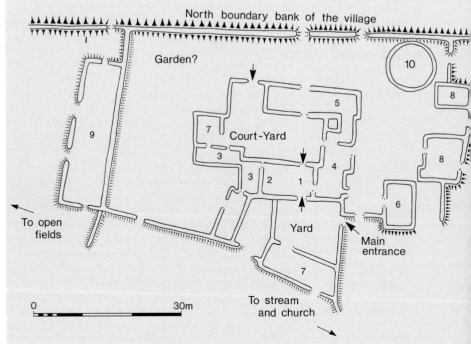

North boundary bank of the village

Garden?

10

8

9

7
Court-Yard

5

3

7

3   2   1

4

8

To open fields

Yard

6

Main entrance

7

0   30m

To stream and church

WRP

North Manor), and the other further south. The traces of buildings and enclosures which can be seen as raised patterns in the turf are very typical of the plan of twelfth and thirteenth century manorial homesteads which survive as standing buildings all over the country. These are very different from simpler peasant houses and have not been excavated. The earthworks suggest varied building shapes: a courtyard surrounded by linked buildings - the hall with solar block (private rooms for the lord's family); the bakehouse and brewery; a separate kitchen block; a circular dovecot; a long barn and

1 Hall: communal eating and meeting area

2 Dais: the high table position

3 Lord of the Manor's private rooms: the 'solar', chapel and bedroom

4 Service rooms: probably used by servants for storage, food preparation, or as sleeping quarters

5 Bakehouse / brewery area: this range may also have contained a steward's house or gatehouse as it is next to the courtyard entrance. The small, square structure may be the base of a stone stair turret

6 Kitchen: separate from the main building to avoid the spread of fire

7 Possibly stabling

8 Buildings associated with farming and feeding the household: tools, poultry, animals, wood for kitchen fire

9 A long barn with entrances on the gable ends and the west side

10 Site of haystack or dovecote

outbuildings for animals, tools and carts. Dips in the wall lines indicate the position of doorways, and the area is defined by boundary banks and well-worn footpaths.

The position of the manor within the village also emphasises its importance. It is on the highest part of the settlement area, and buildings of two or more storeys would have allowed a good view - adding to the commanding and defensible nature of the courtyard plan. A 'sunken way' passes close by, a convenient route to the water supply in the valley, the fields surrounding the village, and beyond towards Kirkham Priory, Malton and York.

Excavations nearby found evidence that people farmed here over 2,000 years ago. The holes and gullies where timbers had been set up for buildings, together with pottery and other objects dating from the centuries before the Roman Conquest show that a large farm stood here during the Iron Age (c700BC to AD50). Occupation continued into the Roman period (AD50-400) - re-used Roman masonry and fragments of window glass suggest that a villa was nearby, although its main buildings have not been found. There was also Saxon occupation. Two buildings measuring only 3.5m x 2.5m with floors cut down below the surrounding ground level and a hole at each end for a post to hold up the roof were constructed in the line of the main east-west routeway.

2 The South Manor

Medieval peasant houses built over the remains of another manor house, and finds from a wealthy Anglo-Saxon and Viking settlement

An area of ground towards the centre of the plateau farmstead sites was chosen for the exploration of a medieval peasant

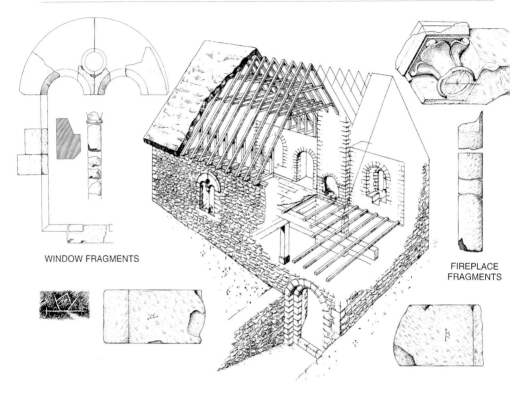

WINDOW FRAGMENTS

FIREPLACE FRAGMENTS

The discovery, in 1955, of the basement of a storeyed building - a late twelfth-century manor house - was the first of many major surprises over the 40 years of excavations at Wharram. Architectural features found in situ included the entrance threshold, three central pillar bases set on the earth floor which would have supported the timber cross-beams of the principal first-floor room, and the base of a fireplace for the same room, all built with dressed sandstone blocks and chalk rubble. Over 250 burnt earthenware tiles, sherds of medieval pottery, and 150 pieces of sandstone had fallen into the basement when the building was being dismantled in around 1250. Parts of windows, carved capitals and column bases, probably the remains of a hooded fireplace, were found, and are shown in this reconstruction drawing. Several pieces of sandstone had a distinctive mason's mark carved at the quarry.

house and its croft. Quite unexpectedly the site of a second manor house, dating from the twelfth and thirteenth centuries, was also found beneath the late medieval peasant house.

The South Manor buildings had been dismantled in the thirteenth century, but what little remained was clearly part of the house of a lord of the manor. The

cellar or 'undercroft' of a late twelfth century two-storey stone building had cornerstones, carved window surrounds and a fireplace of imported sandstone, a great contrast to the peasant houses.

Evidence of other domestic buildings had been quarried away when the site was taken over by tenant farmers in the later thirteenth century, and the only other

P GWILLIAM

Excavations here in the 1980s uncovered Saxon levels dating from c650 - 850 A.D. One of the earliest finds is this coin, a sceat of c700 - 725 A.D., which matches the radio-carbon date for charcoal from the smithy.

remains belonging to the manorial farmstead were a large storage pit, two latrine pits and a circular ditch which probably surrounded a hay stack.

Finds dating from the eighth to the eleventh century prove that this part of the village was the site of an important residence in earlier Anglo-Saxon and Viking times. It was, perhaps, the home of a Saxon thegn (a landowner), taken over and used as a manor house after the Norman Conquest. A building could be identified during excavation by a concentration of post holes. It had obviously once been substantial. Anglo-Saxon objects include iron sword fittings, combs and pins made out of antler or bone, thousands of fragments of pottery vessels, iron knives and copper alloy belt fittings. The thegn had his own smith, and evidence was found for his smithy and

some of the objects he made there. Another important find of metalwork was a pair of copper alloy belt fittings which had been made in Scandinavia around the year 900AD.

3 The Peasant Farmstead

Excavations revealed the houses and lifestyle of peasant farmers during the medieval period

Between 1950 and 1970 several house sites were excavated and a complicated pattern of rebuilding, varied use and changing fortunes was revealed, with tens of thousands of pottery, metal and other objects and animal bones recorded. Research has built up a picture of the type of houses built here, and their contents.

The foundations were of chalk rubble,

These 'Borre' style belt fittings for a leather belt were made in Scandinavia and are clear evidence that the site was occupied continually from the middle Saxon period to Viking times. They probably reached Wharram as part of the clothing of a wealthy Scandinavian settler granted an estate here.

P GWILLIAM

PETER DUNN

IRON KEYS

IRON PADLOCK BOLTS

BRONZE BROOCHES AND BUCKL

HINGE
PIVOT

BONE FLUTE
FRAGMENT

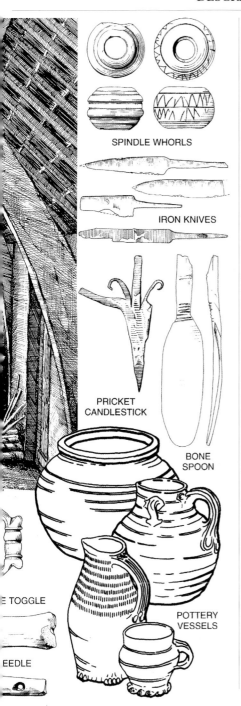

SPINDLE WHORLS

IRON KNIVES

PRICKET CANDLESTICK

BONE SPOON

TOGGLE

POTTERY VESSELS

EEDLE

quarried from within the village area. The walls and roof were formed by curved tree trunks, split lengthwise to make pairs of 'cruck' blades braced by a short horizontal beam forming an 'A' shape, set up to support the roof. Each pair of crucks was linked by straight timbers at head height and above. Straight branches were fastened into horizontal timbers between the crucks, and flexible wattles were interwoven and daubed with soil and lime mixed with water and animal hair; the roof was thatched with reeds or straw. As wind and rain caused the walls and roof to deteriorate, they were repaired without disturbing the cruck blades, which were set into the ground or raised up on stone blocks. If the use of the building changed, the position of the entrance could be moved and the stone foundations rebuilt or taken out to form a new threshold; the house could be lengthened or shortened by adding or removing a pair of crucks.

People depended on their own cows and sheep for food and clothing, and they

A reconstruction of the home of a peasant family in the thirteenth to fifteenth centuries, and some of the finds used to build up a picture of the interior.

The shape of surface earthworks suggest the plan form of a main living area flanked by a store/sleeping room and a byre. Excavations revealed the position of crucks, wall foundations, doorways and fireplace. Floors of packed earth were worn into hollows and most finds were made in the yard areas outside.

Typical finds are illustrated, and include pottery vessels and spindle whorls, iron knives, hooks, hasps, hinges, padlocks, keys and candle sticks. Bone spoons, flutes, toggles and needles, bronze brooches, buckles and rings also survived, often in tiny fragments, to be carefully preserved and reconstructed hundreds of years later.

depended on a single fire for warmth, light and cooking. The animals were a vital commodity to be kept under a watchful eye, their body warmth valuable during the winter. The houses were therefore dual-purpose, housing both people and animals, an entrance area dividing the living and sleeping area from the animals in the byre. The main living room contained the open hearth, and there was perhaps a store or a sleeping room for the head of the household at the end of the building, private, but unheated. Straight trimmed branches or split planks were laid across the rooms at head height to provide storage or sleeping space, but this could not extend across the hearth area unless a timber hood was built to allow smoke to escape.

The wooden parts of the houses and their contents have long gone, but many sherds of pottery and fragments of iron and copper alloy have been pieced together and studied in order to reconstruct the vessels used for food and drink. Other finds include door and window fittings and parts of boxes. Strap hinges probably came from plank doors which had iron hinge pivots set into stone jambs, while other doors were 'harr-hung' - pivotted into a beam at the top and a stone with a hole cut into it at the base. Small strap hinges and hinge pivots suggest that the windows ('wind eyes' to let the smoke out) had wooden shutters to control the draught, and fragments of lead and glass suggest that some windows were glazed.

Small hinges, strips of bronze, keys and padlocks provide evidence of containers which would have kept their contents safe from vermin and thieves. A large chest contained grain, stored before milling into flour for the family's main food - bread; a smaller box held the seed corn and a secure box held money and other valuables. Other boxes would have contained household items such as needles, pins, knives, spoons, combs and game pieces such as dice.

4 The Pond and Water Mill

Water in a sheltered valley - the vital ingredients for a settlement from earliest times

Water is a rare commodity on the Wolds where streams run underground, beneath the chalk. 'The Beck' at Wharram, which runs along the clay valley bottom, is fed by springs, the first of them emerging just below the junction of Deepdale and Drue Dale. The water supply has been controlled by damming since at least the ninth century. The pond so formed would have been the focal point of the village, as people collected water for cooking and washing, brought sheep and cattle and horses here to drink, or fished. The water was controlled by sluices and fed to two mills to power machinery for grinding the corn grown in Wharram's fields.

A revetment of woven branches held the clay dam in position and channels were dug and re-dug to control the water flow. Stone foundations and fragments of millstones of a ninth to eleventh century corn mill were found. Waterlogged conditions preserved part of a wooden shovel blade, fragments of leather shoes and basketwork. Pollen, seeds and beetle remains show that during the early medieval period there were no trees growing near the pond, and that the landscape was arable, with grass. The remains of both plaster and furniture beetles from nearby structures were found in the sediments.

The mill was abandoned in the twelfth or thirteenth century but the pond was stocked with fish during the later Middle Ages by the monks of Haltemprice Priory near Hull. The fourteenth century fishpond was recreated by rebuilding the dam after excavations which revealed that sandstone blocks were used to re-surface the dam in the eighteenth century - work done by the sole remaining tenant farmer or for the parson. Although the farmhouse built then had a stone culvert to carry water from a spring higher up the valley, the pond would still have been an important source of water for animals and the footpath from Thixendale crossed the beck here.

A sheep-wash was built against the dam in the nineteenth century, and the decline in the importance of the springs on this site was complete when in 1935 a collection tank was built and the water pumped to settlements elsewhere.

5 The Church of St Martin, the Graveyard and Vicarage

The water of life - evidence that Wharram was a sacred site before the advent of Christianity

Between 1962 and 1974 the first complete excavation of a rural medieval church in Britain was undertaken here, and archaeologists recorded the complicated changes in its shape and size over a thousand years. Plans, showing its foundation in the tenth century, its development into a large parish church in the fourteenth and then its reduction as the site was deserted, are displayed inside. The medieval church at Wharram was served by a priest who lived nearby, just north of the churchyard.

It is possible that the area occupied by the church and its graveyard had a spiritual significance long before the Christian religion was brought to Wharram. Medieval graves on the north side of the graveyard were dug around a much older burial, possibly originally covered by a mound, which has been dated to the first two centuries BC, suggesting that the place was respected as a place of interment from earlier times. The springs were perhaps originally associated with a pagan water cult, and

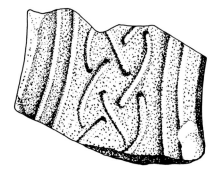

The font from St. Martin's church dates from about AD1200 and is now in the church of St Michael and All Angels, Hull. The last baptism at Wharram was in 1946, a few years before the church was closed as a regular place of worship.

A fragment from the arm of an eighth century sandstone cross carved with a plait-pattern, perhaps a symbol of the Trinity. Only 8cm long, this was found in the filling of a twelfth century ditch on the plateau and had been re-used, and perhaps moved. It may have marked a grave. A fragment of another, undecorated cross of the same date was found near the North Manor.

Wharram Percy in the late twelfth century. All the detail here has been revealed by excavation: the small pond and water mill (bottom right), the Norman church with rounded east end, the peasants' longhouses on the plateau and in the valley beyond the church, and the South Manor house in the distance, right. Changes made by the end of the fourteenth century included the

PETER DUNN

enlargement of the mill pond to the size we see today, the chancel of the church rebuilt without the apse and the graveyard enlarged, and the demolition of the South Manor when the North Manor became the principal house in the village. Throughout the long history and many changes at Wharram Percy one thing remained - the vital water supply in the valley.

then later, when the local leader was converted to Christianity, the water would have been used in the ceremony of baptism.

There was a Christian presence at Wharram Percy from at least the eighth century. The graveyard had reached its full extent by the eleventh century, and by then the first stone church was built at its centre. About a third of the graveyard has been excavated, and nearly 1000 skeletons of men, women and children have been examined, most of them the remains of farmers who lived in the neighbourhood from the eleventh to the sixteenth centuries Most were in simple graves with no grave goods; one exception was the burial of a

Graveslabs Left: an eleventh-century Anglo-Scandinavian slab found in situ. One of a group of three graves (two adults and one child) dug close to the south side of the first stone church on the site. The graves also had head and foot stones broken off at ground level. Centre: a thirteenth-century grave stone carved with the outline of a chalice and a book - the symbols of a priest. No later medieval slabs were found in situ, but many were used in the walls of later phases of the church and several are visible on the south side. Right: a fourteenth-century slab reconstructed from three pieces found in the walls of the church.

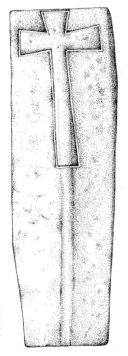
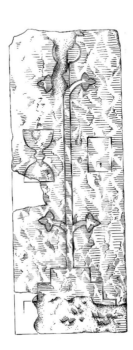
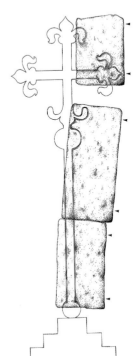

J C THORN

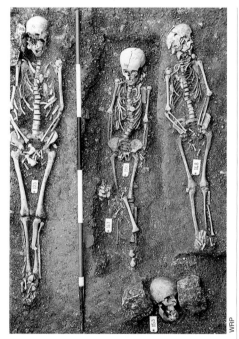

Above: The church and the graveyard ~ nearly 1000 skeletons in over 600 graves were excavated, and many hundreds more rest beneath the turf. In 1000 years of use the early graves were disturbed by later ones as at least four cycles of burial caused the ground level to build up. These medieval skeletons are of a woman in her twenties and children aged about seven and ten.

Top of page: Carved and painted represent-ations of the living and the dead were common in pre-Reformation churches. The carved stone masks illustrated here come from eaves corbels and the ends of mouldings over windows. Some are highly stylised, others are good representations of medieval hair styles and clothing.

priest, with his chalice and patten.

A group of stone grave slabs with crosses carved on them were found on the south side of the chancel, marking the burials of an eleventh-century lord of Wharram and his family. Fragments of broken slabs, carved with crosses and other symbols and dating from the thirteenth and fourteenth centuries, were found built into the walling of the church. But there are no memorials to the bulk of the people buried at Wharram. Only the very wealthy were commemorated in stone, and for most of the (illiterate) population a wooden grave marker, or the tradition of a family burial area within the graveyard, has left no archaeological trace.

Study of the skeletons is still continuing, but much has already been learned about length of life and the diseases people suffered from. Almost half the burials were of babies and children who had probably died of infectious diseases, and their bones show evidence of arrested growth, probably the result of starvation when crops failed because of the harshness of the climate. Their poor diet or periodic food shortages probably account for the fact that children grew slowly, and did not reach today's average heights - an average 15-year-old at Wharram in the fourteenth century would have looked like the average modern 10-year-old. Only about half the babies born here reached their eighteenth birthday, but if people survived that long they then had a 50 per cent chance of reaching 50 or more.

The adult population had to cope with environmental sinusitis - a condition

Reconstruction drawings showing the growth and decline of St Martin's Church.

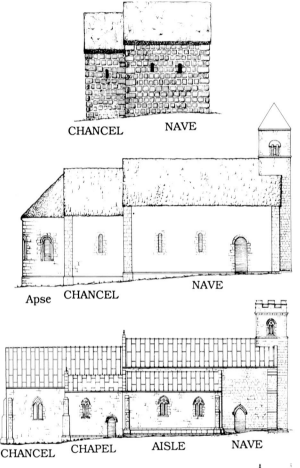

CHANCEL NAVE

Apse CHANCEL NAVE

CHANCEL CHAPEL AISLE NAVE

1000

The excavations revealed the foundations of the small eleventh century church and paving slabs on the present church floor mark their position. The exact nature of the walls and roof is not known, but this drawing gives an impression of its size.

1100 - 1200

Rebuilding probably took place in the twelfth century. This drawing gives an idea of the size of the much larger church which had a west tower and and apsidal east end.

1200 - 1500

The likely appearance of the church by 1450. The apse had been taken down and the chancel made longer; the solid nave walls were pierced by arcading when aisles were built on the south and north sides. A south aisle chapel was built, and in the fifteenth century the whole building was re-roofed and the top stage of the tower rebuilt in its present form.

1500 - 1900

The church we see today. The aisles were demolished in the late fifteenth or early sixteenth century and the arcades blocked; the chancel fell into decay and was rebuilt at a reduced size in the seventeenth century. By the 1950s the building was unused and becoming derelict. Part of the tower collapsed in 1959 and the roof was removed.

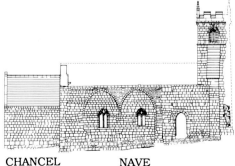

JC THORN

CHANCEL NAVE

which leaves marks on the bone. Chronic infections, from allergies and from animals, and lung diseases such as silicosis have been identified. Bone mineral loss (osteoporosis) occured in women over 50 at a rate similar to today, in spite of the fact that they would have taken in plenty of calcium from the ground water, endured hard physical labour and multiple pregnancies, and (presumably) consumed dairy products from the cows they kept. The resulting fractures visible on these skeletons were crushing of the spine and broken ribs.

There are doubtless many hundreds more graves of Wharram people beneath the turf, as well as the graves of those from the four other townships in the parish. The Church Register records 1200 burials during the 340 years from 1570 to 1910, after the last villager had left. Long after the village had been cleared of living souls, and only the vicarage and a farmhouse were occupied, funeral processions still made the long journey to this isolated spot.

Thirty one gravestones now stand in the area south of the church, most of them dating from the 100 years after 1791. Almost all are of sandstone, probably from the Leeds/Bradford area of the Pennines, and 10 (the earliest of 1820) were carved by stonemasons in Norton, Driffield, Malton and Scarborough. Most of those commemorated were the nineteenth-century 'parish aristocracy' - the wealthier tenant farmers - in an area whose landlords lived in country houses many miles away.

6 The Post-Medieval Vicarage, The New Farmstead and the Remaining Cottages

Only the vicarage and a tenant farm remained in the valley by 1517; sheep grazed on the plateau house sites

Although the village was reduced to a single farmstead by the early sixteenth century, the church continued to be used by the inhabitants of Thixendale, a village two miles away and in the same parish. The vicar lived close to St Martin's until the mid eighteenth century, in a vicarage built around 1554 after a fire. The site can be identified by the cellar which has been left open to view.

By this time the medieval method of farming open fields - the strips of arable cultivated by the villagers - had disappeared; banks with hedges of 'quickwood' (hawthorn) formed the boundaries; common rights and common cultivation had gone. William Botterell was the only farmer living at Wharram Percy in the late seventeenth century; the contents of his house near the vicarage were listed on March 30th 1699, and his house was excavated in 1989. The plan of William's house followed the medieval form of rooms in a line, entered from one another, but now with an upper floor where family members and servants slept, and wool was stored. The farmer's livestock included a flock of sheep, milk cows and eight oxen; there was corn in store, and oats sown in the field, while a waggon, ploughs, harrows and other tools described as 'necessaries belonging husbandrie' were kept in outbuildings.

The 1770s saw a great change in the living standards of both the vicar and the resident farmer: a new parsonage was built by 1770, and a new farmhouse in 1775-9. The parson's new home was not unlike Mr Botterell's house, having three rooms arranged in a straight line, the main living room with a boarded floor raised above the damp ground, and an upper floor. Needles, a thimble and marbles were found where they had dropped between the floorboards. By contrast, the new farmhouse and its

This inventory of 1699 is the earliest documentary evidence for the character and contents of a farmstead at Wharram Percy. The Hearth Tax return shows that William Botterell's farmhouse had a fire-place in three ground floor rooms: his private parlour where he slept and dressed and perhaps had his office; his 'fore room' where he ate and entertained visitors at a table with five chairs and with pewter dishes, plates and tankards in the cupboard; and a kitchen where food was prepared on two tables and cooked in brass 'potts, kettels and pans'. His household items were of little value, but he had considerable wealth in his purse and in the wool and other implements kept in the room over his parlour. The 'wheele' in the fore room was probably a spinning wheel, and his animals were stalled in separate outbuildings.

March 30th 1699 ~

A true Inventary then taken of his Goodes and
chattells moveable and unmoveable of William Botterell
late of Wharham Peircy dec'd
Appraised by us whose names are under written as
follows ~

	£	s	d
In the Parlour			
Inpri's His purse and Apparel	30	00	00
one Bed Bedstead and Bedding	02	10	00
one chest with Linnen	05	10	00
A Table carpett, 3 chaires with other Utensills			
	01	00	00
In the fore Roome			
Eleven pewt. Dishes 6 plates and 2 pewt'Tankerds a			
Chamb'			
= pott salt together with other small peices of pewt.'			
	} 01	10	00

		ts	in
A cupboard Table Wheele 5 chaires & other Implem' there/			
		01	10	00
In the Kitchin			
A Brass potts kettells panns & other small peices ofthe			
same mettall		} 03	10	00
two Tables with other Implem'ts		00	10	00
In the milk house			
one Kimling churns Bowles with other wood vessell			
		01	15	00
In ye fore chamb.'			
Two Beds Bedsteads with Beding and other small			
Utensills therein		09	01	00
In the Parlour Chamb'			
Wooll and other Implem'ts		51	00	00
In the Kitchin Chamb'			
A servants Bed and Beding with other Implem.ts			
therein		01	03	04

spacious outbuildings were built in the most modern style, reflecting eighteenth-century changes in farming practice. The plan has been marked out on the south side of the cottages: it was two rooms deep, with extra rooms for labourers, servants, and storage. The walls were built of the traditional chalk and sandstone, but the front and south walls were faced in brick. The line of a stone conduit which brought water from springs higher up the valley is marked by stones. It was dug through the churchyard, disturbing the bones of generations who had walked to the stream for water.

New fields were now established, with crop rotations to improve the husbandry of sheep and corn. Timber posts and rail fences, planted with ash trees, formed the boundaries to the fields where turnips, corn and hay were grown. Livestock consisted of sheep, cattle and horses, the latter replacing the oxen used to pull the ploughs and carts in earlier times.

The cottages, the only domestic building now standing at Wharram, originated as outbuildings to the 1775 farmhouse. The foundations of other farm buildings can be seen around a courtyard to the north. The new farm layout lasted less than 80 years, for between 1846 and 1851 it was demolished. A new farm, 'High House', (now Wharram Percy farm) was built one mile to the south-west, and the barn became 'Low House' after conversion to cottages. The reason for the removal of the farming centre was probably the inconvenient location of the Wharram farm. The movement of animals and machinery along the ancient hollow way would have been difficult, and the confined nature of the farm site prevented expansion.

While the farm was being taken down there was more disturbance in this quiet valley - in 1847 the construction of the railway line from Malton to Driffield was begun. A small shanty town sprang up on the wold above the valley, and by 1851- the time of the census - 136 navvies were living there in 21 temporary huts.

One hundred years later the valley was once more disturbed by the sound of shovelling and barrowing as archaeologists began their long investigation into its quiet past.

Site Plan and Quick Tour

Section numbers correspond to the main text and to the plan.

1 The tour begins at the north end of the village, on the earthworks of the twelfth and thirteenth-century North Manor. Its site stands beside the easiest climb from the stream to the plateau - a sunken way in use since the Iron Age and which continues west towards Malton and south to Thixendale. The earthworks are identified on the plan. Walk south, along the edge of the plateau and across the low banks which divide the gardens and yards of the medieval peasant houses.

2 The position of part of the South Manor is marked on the ground. The hollows are the traces of chalk quarries, the stone used for building or fertilizer. To the west the archaeologists found the site of an extensive Anglo-Saxon farmstead. Several hollow-ways link the plateau houses to the water supply and main routeway in the valley.

3 The outlines of two medieval peasant houses are marked out on the ground, near the edge of the plateau opposite the church tower. The earliest two-room house dates from the thirteenth century and the longer house, with a living room, inner store room and byre, is fifteenth century. It is the typical medieval house plan built by the peasants with materials obtained nearby, and the earthworks of many more can be seen on the plateau and in the valley.

4 From the plateau the pond is clearly visible, with the old path to Thixendale, now a footpath, crossing the dam. The pond is a reconstruction of the fourteenth century fish pond, with its dam built over the remains of the Saxon mill.

5 Follow the path from the dam to the church. Inside the church an outline of the tenth-century stone church is marked on the floor, and changes in the shape and size of the building are indicated on the plans. The blocked arches of the north and south aisles can be seen on the outside of the building, and the south wall stonework includes fragments of medieval graveslabs.

6 The site of the medieval vicarage and those of the sixteenth and eighteenth centuries lie to the north of the church. Beyond them the site of the farm built in the 1770s, the last farmhouse built at Wharram Percy, is set out in front of the cottages. The cottages were converted from part of the 1770s outbuilding and were last occupied by the Glasspool and Milner families. The building became the headquarters of the Wharram Percy excavations until 1990. The courtyard of the farm buildings stood on the north side. The footpath back towards the car-park crosses the crofts of medieval houses in the valley bottom.

Further reading

Users of this guide are referred to *Wharram Percy Deserted Medieval Village* by Maurice Beresford and John Hurst, published for English Heritage by Batsford Ltd in 1990, ISBN 0-7134-6114-4.